Conducting a Paranormal Investigation

A Training Guide

by Beth Brown

Published by:
IRON CAULDRON BOOKS
Richmond, Virginia
www.ironcauldronbooks.com

International Standard Book Number: 978-0-6152-0456-7

For additional copies or for information about special discounts for bulk purchases, please contact the author directly at:

Beth@Beth-Brown.com

This book is dedicated to my Mom for nurturing my interests, no matter how off-beat, and to my Dad for directing my attention to "the Other Side". I cannot thank either of you enough.

Table of Contents

Introduction

Congratulations! You've taken the first step towards building your credibility as a paranormal researcher – educating yourself about the steps and procedures necessary to collect and support scientifically stable evidence of the existence of the human personality beyond the body. Starting with a good foundation of careful interviewing, detailed site research, and creating a plan for your investigation will help you to establish your reputation as an expert in your field.

Sure, hunting for proof of the paranormal is a fun and exhilarating hobby. Don't forget, though, that taking care of your evidence after your investigation, analyzing the data, and advising sometimes frantic homeowners and other distraught individuals is WORK that can often span weeks or months. These post-hunt steps are arguably the most important aspects of investigating haunted sites and should be taken very seriously. NEVER agree to an investigation unless you are willing to dedicate yourself to completing the data analysis and follow-up.

Because of the rapidly changing nature of paranormal research, this guide does not cover the operation of the equipment you may choose to gather data or detailed methods for analyzing collected data. I encourage you to keep up with current techniques in the field by consulting the internet and new releases from paranormal publishers for further reading and study.

So, do you think you're ready to get out in the field and track down some ghosts? There are a few things you'll need to take care of first...

Getting Permission

The first step in conducting an investigation is finding a site to investigate. A lot of times, leads for locations will come to you through friends or family, but other times you'll have to go out and beat the bushes to find a suspected haunt.

If you will be investigating a public place, be sure to do so only during operating hours unless you have specific **written** permission. Private land always requires the same **written** permission. You should keep a copy of that agreement with you at all times, both on public and private property, in the event you need to show law enforcement officials proof that your visit is approved.

Do not trespass! I cannot stress this point enough. Respect for both public and private property will help you build a good reputation as a paranormal investigator within your community. You will be much more likely to obtain permission to investigate haunted places if you do not have a record for trespassing.

Researching a Haunted Location

Taking all of the various ghost hunting techniques into consideration, I firmly believe that the best foundation for any paranormal investigation is thorough research of the haunted location. History offers us many clues about the possible causes of specific haunts and can help to add weight and credibility to all kinds of strange findings you may come across in the field. Does the site have a tragic past? Was there some other sort of emotional event that occurred there? Not all ghosts linger because of negative reasons, some may have just been so content with life as it was that they don't feel the need to move on. You can almost always narrow down the source of a haunt doing careful research.

Public records are one of the most helpful places to begin your search. You can often find the names of all of a property's previous owners, sometimes dating back hundreds of years. Try searching those names in your town's newspaper archives or through a local historical society. You may uncover some long-forgotten secrets that could help you determine the "who" and "why" behind a haunted location.

Don't overlook or underestimate the **public library** as a source of useful clues. While the internet has helped tremendously with some forms of information gathering, not everything on the web is reliable. Chances are good that if you've heard local ghost stories by word of mouth that someone has documented the tale and hopefully done quite a bit of research on the location already. Sometimes the information found in local libraries is all you need to fill in the holes in your background study, but more often than not it provides only a firm starting point.

You may be surprised what you can find out just by **asking the neighbors** of your suspected haunt! Approaching people in a friendly and honest way generally prompts a positive response and folks will open up with all kinds of stories. Elderly residents may even be able to provide clues where all other sources have fallen short, especially in rural areas where public records were often lost or damaged in small courthouses.

Interviewing Occupants and Witnesses

After your initial contact with the occupants, employees, or visitors of your haunted location, you should schedule a time for a more in-depth interview to obtain details about the witnesses' state of mind and their experiences. Interviews can be successfully conducted by phone, but face-to-face talks often reveal many things via body language (both positive and negative) that a telephone interview cannot. Schedule about one hour for a face-to-face interview and slightly less for a telephone interview.

Have your list of standard interview questions prepared and be sure to read through them to familiarize yourself well ahead of time in case your witness asks you to elaborate or explain something. Interviews should either be documented using an audio recording device or by writing the witness's responses down as they respond. If you chose to write, which is often preferred by those being interviewed as it lessens their "stage fright", let your witness know that you'll be moving along slowly so that you can be sure to capture all of the details of their responses.

If your witness displays any strange behavior or apprehension towards certain interview questions, be sure to make a note AFTER the interview. While most people are truthful and genuinely want to see progress made in your investigation, others are not. Some people are eager for attention or may just want to have a little fun at your expense. Use your instincts and weed out these leads before too much of your group's valuable time is spent on a wild goose chase.

Surveying the Site

Try to either obtain a floor plan of your haunted location or visit the site and draw up your own sketch **in advance**. The size and layout of the site determine the efficiency and maneuverability of the researchers attending the investigation. A good rule of thumb is to have no more than one investigator for every 200 square feet of structure. (Example: a maximum of 6 investigators for a 1200 square ft. home) Go over the floor plan with your team before the investigation and discuss the duties of each researcher and the portion of property on which to focus. Careful preparation at this stage can make all the difference in the outcome of the investigation and the growing reputation of your team!

What to Pack

Your choice of investigational equipment is entirely up to you. You should, of course, pack extra cassettes, memory cards, or CDs that your gear may require.

Here we'll focus on those common-sense things that often go overlooked. Keep a checklist handy while packing your vehicle and be sure to bring:

- Your Permission Letter
- Signed liability forms for the property owner/manager
- Signed confidentiality forms (sometimes required for high-profile city landmarks and other public places)
- Extra batteries - enough for AT LEAST one change in EVERY piece of equipment you bring.

- TWO flashlights. That's one to use and one "just in case."
- A mobile phone. You never know when you may need to call someone's emergency contact, law enforcement, or the paramedics.
- A means of communication other than a mobile phone (examples: short wave radio, CB, family radios, walkie-talkies, etc.) in case of poor or no cellular coverage.
- AT LEAST one bottle of water.
- A first-aid kit.
- A map of the area or GPS in case you get turned around in the dark.

Safety

When preparing for a field investigation, remember that your safety and that of your team members should be your top priority. Dressing for the weather and wearing appropriate shoes for navigating all types of terrain fall into the category of safety and must not be overlooked. If possible, bring along a backpack containing a first-aid kit and a few bottles of water from the list above. Take my husband's motto and make it yours: "It's always better to have them and not need them than to need them and not have them."

Another important item that is often forgotten is some means of communication other than a mobile phone. Lots of haunts are in remote areas that may not have cell coverage for miles around. Family radios and long range walkie-talkies are great for communication between team members and can even play a role in signaling possible paranormal activity by making unexplained chirps and beeps (yes, it's happened to me!)

Don't forget – the safety of your team is a group responsibility! If you see someone putting themselves in harm's way, don't be shy about asking them to play it safe.

Setting Up

Setting up your investigations takes practice – you'll learn a better, faster way to do something each time and (hopefully) also learn from previous mistakes.

Take the time BEFORE splitting your group into smaller teams or placing stationary equipment to check for environmental factors that may contaminate your evidence. Nearby power lines, fuse boxes, microwave ovens (both off and on), and even household dimmer switches can distort EMF readings. Excessive dust, moisture, or mold can create false positives in photographs by causing reflections or orbs. Wind whistling through attic vents has been known to cause wailing and crying sounds in audio recordings. Use your detective skills and look and listen to your surroundings with scrutiny. Make notes of ANY potential contaminants and their location – the time you spend writing these things down at the start of your investigation could mean the difference between obtaining valuable data that is considered proof of paranormal activity and having questionable data that has to be thrown out. Cover all of your bases early!

Since you have already studied the floor plan or map of the area you're about to investigate, you should know the best way to divide your team to effectively cover the site. Set up any stationary equipment and test that it is working properly before starting your walk-through. A few extra minutes of recorded data can provide a great payoff.

It is best that buildings being investigated are free from pets, children, and any spectators that may want to study your group and their methods. Anyone who has ever attempted to collect audio evidence in a crowded house can tell you that it is nearly impossible to analyze their recordings to search for paranormal interference. If possible, notify the occupants of the building in advance of these concerns and ask that they only have ONE other person besides themselves present for the investigation.

Outdoor locations, especially those open to the public, will be challenging to investigate regardless of your attempts to isolate yourself from manmade noises. It is helpful, though, to make a statement in your recording about the conditions of your surroundings. Are there four people about a hundred yards from you? Say so. You're fifty feet from a highway? Tell your recorder!

If you are participating in an **active investigation**, you're ready to proceed with your walk-through. If you are participating in a **passive investigation**, now is the time to activate your motion-sensing equipment or place your perimeter seals (tape, thread, etc) to secure the area and announce to your recording equipment that your team is leaving the site. Talking to your gear may sound silly now, but it will prove very helpful when you are reviewing your evidence later.

Active Investigations

Active investigations are those in which the investigators move about the site to collect photo, video, audio, thermal, and electronic data. Often there is some sort of attempt at communication with entities, such as asking questions during audio recordings or asking an entity to make itself visible while the team takes photographs.

Provide each team member with an Activity Log to jot down the types of phenomena, if any, that they witness and the time. If using an EMF meter, make a note of any high or unusual readings during the walk-through on the Activity Log. These reports can often help to offer clues to anomalies in photographs or audio recordings.

The benefits of an active investigation are that you can potentially "stir up" paranormal responses and can experience olfactory and other phenomena that cannot be recorded. The downside of this approach is the amount of "trash" noise created by investigators (footsteps, coughing, etc.) that you'll need to wade through during your data analysis. I've also found that some people tend to feed off of the excitement or fear of others and will start hearing or seeing what is suggested to them. Be careful to keep your wits – no matter what!

Passive Investigations

Passive investigations are those in which equipment is set up and left to record an unoccupied building or outdoor site. There is no attempt at communication with entities.

The benefits of a passive investigation are the clean quality of the data collected and the "tamper resistant" boundary (perimeter alarms, tape, threads, flour, etc.) placed on the site. Carefully collected evidence gathered in controlled conditions carries far more weight than a frame or two of questionable footage caught by a shaky video camera in a room full of people. The downside of this approach is that you have no opportunity to try and motivate the potential source of paranormal activity to speak or materialize and you cannot record scent or touch phenomena.

Investigation Etiquette

Much like attending a movie theatre or five-star restaurant, there are several rules of etiquette that should be followed while participating in a paranormal investigation. Many of them are to ensure an efficient and safe investigation process, but others are critical for the collection of clean, uncontaminated evidence.

- **Do not whisper.** Whispering can make it nearly impossible to differentiate between paranormal interference and the voices of team members in audio data. Try and train yourself to always speak at your conversational volume. Use your ears to investigate your surroundings and help your team to do the same by keeping verbal communication at a minimum.
- **Do not smoke.** Particles in cigarette smoke can carry much farther than we are able to detect with our naked eye but often result in false ectoplasmic mists in

photographs. It is also thought that the scents of cigar and cigarette smoke are a signal from spirits that they are near.

- **Do not wear perfume.** Again, it is thought that floral scents are a signal of the presence of spirits – try not to confuse your team by bathing in heavily fragranced products or misting on cologne or perfume before an investigation.
- **Keep your flashlight pointed at the ground.** Blinding your teammates with a flashlight beam can cause them to trip and fall, lose their bearings, or even miss a visual paranormal event. Using glow sticks is often a good solution to prevent "eye-shine" during interior investigations, but headlamps in any environment tend to only make the problem worse.
- **Watch that flash!** Be careful when taking photographs to warn any team members that may be in the shot to shield or close their eyes. Optical recovery from a camera flash can sometimes take three minutes or more and can cause the same problems as an ill-aimed flashlight.
- **Keep your cool.** Mentally prepare yourself ahead of time for the investigation and think about how you might react to a startling or unbelievable event. Screaming and running are not usually your best options!

Breaking Down

I know that it is easy to get carried away by the rush of an exciting investigation. Packing up can seem like a simple task – turn off your equipment and toss it into a bag, right? WRONG! Do not waste all of your painstaking preparation time by making a careless mistake when wrapping up the period of evidence collection.

The first step of breaking down a passive investigation is to check all of your perimeter or boundary alarms for tampering. Next, if motion sensors were used, make note of any units that were tripped and their location. For both passive and active investigations, make an audible statement that you are concluding your evidence collection and the time so that it may be captured by your recording devices. Switch off all of your video cameras and audio recorders.

Take care to pack all of your equipment away safely to preserve your new harvest of data. A hard-sided, waterproof, lockable case is ideal for transporting valuable electronics and for preserving delicate recorded media. Another safety measure that can also help to add another level of credibility to your evidence is to always keep your gear and any memory cards, cassette tapes, and DVDs with you at all times if possible.

Once your gear is packed, have at least two team members do final sweeps of the site to assure that nothing has been left behind. ALWAYS leave as a site exactly as you found it!

Make multiple copies of ALL of your collected evidence as soon as possible, preferably the same day as your investigation. Sadly, evidence that is not backed up almost always meets with an unfortunate fate.

Data Analysis

Begin the long and often tedious process of reviewing your evidence as soon as possible following your investigation so the events of the day or evening are still fresh in your mind. Allow yourself plenty of rest, though, between your visit to the investigation site and the start your data review – you don't want adrenaline tainting your view of things and making you see or hear things that may not be there.

Dividing the duty of evidence review between team members makes the process much faster. It also helps to have several people working independently with the same information to see what each will discover. Some investigators are better at analyzing sound files while others may be able to easily spot "true" orbs in photographs and video. You and your teammates will discover your individual talents in time and should separate the evidence according to the proficiencies of each.

Keep careful logs of your analyzed data. Note the time of suspect sounds in audio recordings. Jot down anything you may remember from the moments surrounding an anomalous photo. Save copies of your questionable findings in a separate file to aid in preparation of your group's concluding report and to share with occupants or managers of the site you investigated.

Time is very important at this stage in the research process – your "client" will likely be quite anxious to learn of your results. Practice will improve your efficiency without affecting the quality of your final report, but until you've gone through the investigation process from start to finish several times, take your time and be thorough with EVERYTHING. Remember, you're building your credibility and your reputation in the paranormal community!

Analyzing Photos

If you're lucky, you'll notice at least one of three suspect things in photographs from your investigation: mists, light points, or orbs.

Mists are exactly what they sound like – foggy, shapeless masses that appear in photos but were not seen with the naked eye. I always try and rule out anything that may have caused the effect at the scene, like breath on cool days and nights, smoke, or vehicle exhaust. If you can eliminate those possibilities as the cause of the mist captured in a photo, chances are good that you have something paranormal on your hands.

This is an excellent example of a mist that even appears to "glow".

Light points, a harsh bright spot of light that seems to produce its own glow, is a photo anomaly seen slightly more often than mists. To be sure that you have a true light point, you must first check that there are no reflections of the sun bouncing off of anything in your surroundings. I've found that taking multiple photos in the same place and in the same position is a good way to narrow down what is environmental light and what is otherwise unexplainable. After you've assessed the lights caused by reflections of the sun, make sure you are not causing the flash of your camera to bounce off of any glass or other highly polished surface. If you're shooting in the daylight, do so without a flash. If you are shooting at night or in dimly lit interiors, try using a flash filter to soften the light and to reduce glare and reflections.

An orb seems to have captured the dog's attention.

Finally, the most commonly seen and the most commonly debated photo anomaly is the orb. **Orbs** are rings of light with softly glowing centers that look very much like a bubble. Scientists, photography experts, and seekers of the paranormal all have different theories as to what orbs could be. Some scientists believe that the broad spectrum of light captured by digital cameras, much greater than human eyes can detect, is somehow capturing an image of invisible earth energies similar to magnetic fields.

Photography experts tend to lean towards dust as the main cause of orbs in photos, but cannot explain why orbs appear only *sometimes* in dusty locations.

Paranormal researchers seem to be rather accepting of the idea that spirit energy leaves the human body at death and takes on the most simple of physical forms, the sphere. This theory is usually accompanied by the beliefs that these balls of spirit energy are often moving too fast to be seen with the naked eye and that they only reflect tiny amounts of the light spectrum – those just beyond our naturally visible range.

One thing they all seem to agree on is that none can state that their theory is any more than that – a theory. Personally, I figure I have all of my bases covered with my belief that not all spirits are orbs and not all orbs are spirits. I prefer to examine each on a case by case basis and compare each photo containing orbs to other photos taken at the same time and place and encourage you to do the same. A scrutinizing eye is a paranormal investigator's best asset.

Analyzing Audio

EVP is the shortened name for a startling discovery in the field of paranormal research known as "Electronic Voice Phenomena." Disembodied voices that are unheard by human ears at the time of the recording but are audible during its playback are referred to as EVP.

The recording of messages from the spirit world using electronic devices got its start quite by accident. In 1959, Fredrich Jurgenson of Sweden made a recording of birds singing in their natural habitat. When he played back the track of bird songs, he heard the voice of a man speaking Norwegian talking about the sounds of nocturnal birds. Amazed at his discovery, Jurgenson continued making similar recordings and amassed a large number of tracks with disembodied voices over a relatively short period of time.

Jurgenson's collection caught the attention of Latvian psychologist, Konstantin Raudive. Raudive began researching the capture of these mysterious voices in a much more controlled laboratory setting and managed to record over 100,000 messages during his twenty years of work. Raudive published his findings in his 1971 book *Breakthrough*. He is still today considered the pioneer of EVP research.

So, where are these voices coming from and why can we only hear them when they're recorded? Research, having exhausted every other logical explanation, points to the messages coming from spirits of the dead. It is believed that, while inaudible to the living, spirits are somehow able to manipulate the recording media to create an imprint of their voice or other sounds such as scrapes, knocks, or crashes. Decades of study, however, have yet to determine how exactly spirits are able to achieve this feat.

Well, couldn't you just be picking up pieces of a radio or television broadcast and misinterpreting it to be a message from "the other side?" That is certainly a legitimate assumption, but EVP researchers have found that they can block those broadcast signals, using Faraday Cages and other devices, and still produce the same results. Also consider that the messages received are often a direct response to questions asked by those making the recordings. Can a TV or radio broadcast do that?

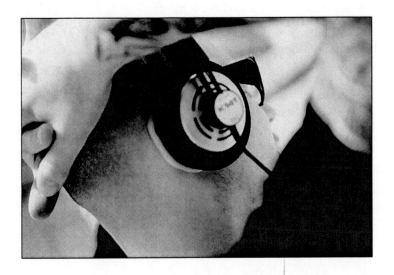

Like all aspects of paranormal research, Electronic Voice Phenomena is still a form of evidence that is surrounded by questions and is the topic of much debate. As science and technology have progressed and made recording devices quite inexpensive and easy to use, EVP has been embraced by thousands in search of the paranormal and by those seeking messages of comfort from loved ones that have passed. My feeling is that when we've answered all of the questions we have on the subject of EVP, mankind will likely have already found its "proof" and the quest for confirmation of an afterlife will be over.

Until such a breakthrough in EVP research is made, I encourage you to collect audio data for yourselves and consider it as a possible method of spirit communication. As with photographic evidence, every attempt must be made to ensure that the recorded phenomena are not caused by "natural" things in the surrounding area.

EVP are categorized based on audible clarity and the amount of "tweaking" that is done to a recording in order to hear the anomaly. When analyzing your own audio data, you can refer to these classifications to prioritize and log your findings:

Classification A EVP -
"A clear and distinct voice or sound that is universally accepted and undisputed, because it must be understood by anyone with normal hearing and without being told or prompted to what is being said or heard. It can be heard without the use of headphones."

Classification B EVP -
"A voice or sound that is distinct and fairly loud. This class of voice is more common and can be heard by most people after being told what to listen for. It is usually audible to experienced persons who have learned the skill of listening to EVP. It can sometimes be heard without the use of headphones."

Classification C EVP -
"A faint and whispery voice or sound that can barely be heard and is sometimes indecipherable and unintelligible. It may have paranormal characteristics, such as a mechanical sound. Most investigators would apply objectivity and disregard it, but may save it for reference purposes."

Putting It All Together

So, you've assembled your suspicious evidence and picked it apart to rule out any possible natural causes. Now it's time to get your team together and discuss the entire COLLECTION of findings and try and come to a conclusion whether the cause of your anomalous data is paranormal. Believe me, it is not often an easy task. There will always be a "what if it was ____?" or "it might have been ____" that will leave you leaning to the natural side of things. That's our logical human mind at work – and that's a good thing because it keeps us in check. If you start seeing evidence of spirits everywhere you look, you're probably only seeing what you *want* to see.

Let's say your team found ten anomalies in your photos and audio. Three of those findings were questionable and *may* have been caused by investigator error or some environmental factor. Seven of your findings, however, remain unexplainable by known science. Chances are good that you have revealed true paranormal activity!

If those numbers were reversed, seven findings were questionable and only three remained unexplained, the chances of their being caused by paranormal activity are drastically lowered. This will ONLY hold true if your team is methodical, experienced, and careful in its evidence collection. Investigator errors can often cause true paranormal activity to go undetected. Practice is the only thing that will assure you get optimum results from every investigation!

Advising Clients About Your Conclusions

After all of the excitement of a paranormal investigation and the thrill of reviewing your evidence, don't forget why you started the process. If a client contacted you out of fear or concern about events in their home, it is your responsibility as an investigator to communicate your findings in a clear, calm manner free from jargon. Show them your evidence and explain how your group drew its conclusions. Answer the client's questions honestly and NEVER be afraid to admit that you don't know something. You can always say, "I'm not sure I have all of the information I'd need to give you the best answer, but I'd be happy to research it and get back to you." Remember , your credibility is very valuable.

Has your team come to the conclusion that something paranormal is at the root of the client's problems? What now? Homeowners will often ask for your help or advice on how to "get rid of" the spirits that are troubling them. Have a list of specialists ready, based on information about the client's belief system established early on in your preliminary interview, in that specific area of spiritual cleansing that are willing to work with the client at this point.

Often, clients are simply curious about the events they've witnessed and are seeking only some kind of acknowledgment of their sanity. Many will show relief when you share your anomalous findings with them and say things like, "Wow! You mean I'm not crazy?" Be prepared for anything – I've seen all kinds of reactions!

Someone on your team with a background in customer service or sales may be a good candidate to conduct the post-investigation presentation. They usually have had extensive practice in explaining products or processes to those that have no prior knowledge of their workings. They also are well adept at handling various emotional responses from clients and keeping the situation calm and comfortable. These skills, though, can be learned by any team member and honed through role-playing practice and case experience.

Case Closed

When can you close a case? Never, really. You may close one only to reopen it again and again.

If strange things have been reported to occur regularly at the location of your investigation, they will probably continue. A client may contact you from time to time to discuss recent activity or even request that your team make a return visit because of new or different suspected paranormal events at the site. You should consider this a compliment – your team has likely made a favorable impression by conducting themselves as professionals!

Resources

Appendix A
Sample Interview Questions

Feel free to copy or modify these questions to best suit the research methods of your investigative team.

1. Address of site:

2. Name of witness:

3. Mailing address if different:

4. Phone number:

5. Email Address:

6. Number of occupants at location:

7. Number of pets:

8. Occupants' names and ages:

9. Occupants' occupations:

10. Occupants' religious beliefs:

11. Time of occupancy at the location:

12. Age of the site:

13. How many previous owners? (if known):

14. History of site: (tragedies, deaths, previous complaints)

15. How many rooms in the site?

16. Has the location been blessed?

17. Has there been any recent remodeling? (if so, what and

where):

18. Are any occupants on prescribed medication? (anxiety, depression, pain, etc) Please list names and medications:

19. Are any occupants using illegal drugs? (this will be kept confidential):

20. Do any occupants drink alcohol heavily? (this will be kept confidential):

21. Are any occupants interested in the occult? (Ouija, séances, psychics, spells) If so, who and what?

22. Are any occupants currently seeing a psychiatrist or in therapy? (this will be kept confidential) If so, who:

23. Any occupants with frequent or unexplained illnesses? (if yes, describe):

24. Have any religious clergy been consulted? If so, please list church:

25. Has there been any media involvement? If so, who/when:

26. Have there been any other witnesses besides the occupants? (names and relationships)

27. Have there been any odors? (i.e. perfumes, flowers, sulfur, ammonia, excrement, etc) If so, when, where and what:

28. Have there been any sounds? (i.e. footsteps, knocks,

banging, etc) If so, when, where and what:

29. Have there been any voices? (whispering, yelling, crying, speaking) If so, when, where and what:

30. Has there been any movement of objects? If so, when, where and what?

31. Have there been any apparitions? If so, when, where and what (describe the apparition)?

32. Have there been any uncommon cold or hot spots? If so, when, where and what?

33. Have there been any problems with electrical appliances? (TV, lights, kitchen appliances, doorbells) If so, when, where and what?

34. Have there been any problems with plumbing? (leaks, flooding, sinks, toilet bowls) If so, when, where and what?

35. Any occupants having nightmares or trouble sleeping? If so, who and when?

36. Has there been any physical contact? If so, who, where and what happened?

37. Are pets affected? If so, how?

38. Describe the first occurrence of the phenomena: (what and when happened?)

39. Who first witnessed the phenomena?

40. What time was the first occurrence of the phenomena?

41. Were there any other witnesses during the first event?

42. How long is the average duration of the phenomena?

43. How often do the phenomena occur?

44. Do any of the occupants feel the phenomena are threatening: If so, who and why?

45. Do all of the occupants agree on what is happening? Do any think the events are nonsense or not happening?

46. What would you like to see accomplished from our visit?

Appendix B
Site Access Agreement

Modify this sample and print two copies on your organization's letterhead. Have both copies signed and retain one for your records. Keep a photocopy of this document with you at all times during your investigation!

I, the undersigned, have the authority to grant access to the (Your Group Name) Investigation Team members and affiliated persons to the below listed location for the purpose of conducting an investigation and/or conducting field research into possible paranormal or unexplained events.

The investigation process has been explained to me and I give the (Your Group Name) Investigation Team permission to conduct an investigation and/or research at this location, with restriction(s) if noted.

The (Your Group Name) Investigation Team releases the owner/operator of the location from any liabilities for any injuries and/or equipment damages that may occur during the investigation.

The (Your Group Name) Team assumes full responsibility for our actions and for any damages to the property during the investigation.

I understand and acknowledge that the (Your Group Name) Investigation Team will never trespass or intentionally damage property. I affirm that I am authorizing this investigation of my own free will and that the services and time of the (Your Group Name) Investigation Team are free of any cost, charge, or fee.

Grantor: Signature:
Date/Time Investigation Permitted:
Restrictions:

Team Leader: Signature:

Appendix C
Investigation Activity Log

Investigator Name:
Date: Time:
Location:
Site Contact:
Weather Conditions:

<u>Equipment Present:</u>

Digital Camera   Standard Camera (type: _____ mm)
EMF Meter   Non-Contact Thermometer
Digital Audio Recorder   Analog Audio Recorder
Digital Video Camera   Analog Video Camera
Other:_____
Other:_____
Other:_____

Phenomenon Experienced:	Time:

Recommended Websites

www.ghostvillage.com
Author Jeff Belanger's home of the paranormal. Features of the site include a regular web-radio broadcast, article archives, and reader submissions of personal paranormal experiences.

www.hollowhill.com/guide/guide.htm
Hollow Hill has an excellent collection of articles about ghost-hunting and paranormal research. Check out their online guide for ghost-hunters!

www.hauntedtimes.com
Haunted Times Magazine is a great place to keep up with industry news, convention announcements, and technical information about popular gear.

www.apsrradio.com
APSR Paranormal Talk Radio Show, is a part of the Alabama ParaSpiritual Research Radio Network (APSRNetwork) that brings Paranormal Talk Radio shows from around the world. APSR Broadcasting & Productions hosts shows like: APSR Paranormal Talk Radio, Shadowtalk Paranormal Talk Radio, and Paranormal Divas Talk Radio Show. Encore Shows play 24/7 except when live shows are airing.

www.newenglandparanormal.com/learn/learn_7.htm
New England Paranormal has provided this excellent resource for those hoping to learn more about photographing spirits.

Bibliography

Danelek, J. Allan. *The Case for Ghosts*. Llewellyn Publications, Woodbury, MN, 2006.

Jones, Marie D. *PSIence: How New Discoveries in Quantum Physics and New Science May Explain the Existence of Paranormal Phenomena.* New Page Books, Franklin Lake, NJ, 2006.

LeShan, Lawrence L. *The World of the Paranormal: The Next Frontier*. Helios Press, New York, NY, 2004.

Stoeber, Michael F. *Critical Reflections of the Paranormal*. State University of New York Press, Albany, NY, 1996.

About the Author

Beth Brown's search for proof of the paranormal began in 1989 and her quest ultimately led to her founding the Virginia Society of Paranormal Education and Research in 2007. She is the author of *Haunted Battlefields: Virginia's Civil War Ghosts*, the upcoming *Haunted Plantations of Virginia*, a cookbook - *From a Witch's Kitchen: Celebrating Seasonal Magic in Every Meal*, plus many articles about the technical aspects of ghost-hunting and her city's colorful history. Beth lives with her husband, daughter, son, two cats, two dogs, and a handful of spirits in Richmond, Virginia.

You can keep up with her current work at:
www.Beth-Brown.com

CPSIA information can be obtained at www.ICGtesting.com
Printed in the USA
LVOW060418110413

328422LV00002B/485/P